Flickering
Foundations

Noel and Denise Enete

WAVE
Study
Bible

Published by WAVE Study Bible, Inc., *wavestudybible.com*
Available from Amazon, *amazon.com*
Edition 1.0.0

Scripture quotations noted **NIV** are taken from the *HOLY BIBLE, NEW INTERNATIONAL VERSION*. Copyright 1973, 1978, and 1984 by International Bible Society. Used by permission of Zondervan Publishing House. All rights reserved.

Scripture quotations noted **NASB** are taken from the *NEW AMERICAN STANDARD BIBLE*, Copyright 1960, 1962, 1963, 1968, 1971, 1972, 1973, 1975, 1977, by The Lockman Foundation. Used by permission.

The FLCR study strategy was adapted from Anne Graham Lotz's *Living a Life that is Blessed*, Copyright 1995 by AnGel Ministries.

ISBN 978-0-9791595-4-1

Printed and bound in the United States of America

Table of Contents

"More than half of every practice was spent on fundamental drills."

John Wooden

Preface

Possibly the best coach of all time was UCLA's John Wooden, "The Wizard of Westwood," who coached basketball for the Bruins from 1948 to 1975. Besides his unequaled winning record (10 national championships in a 12 year period) he is also known for his belief in practicing the fundamentals. Many people are surprised to learn that more than half of every one of his practices was spent working on fundamental drills, even the last practice of the season. He believed that continuing to practice the fundamentals put you in the best place to have success in the game.

There are also fundamentals in the Christian life. These are not elemental concepts that the seasoned believer outgrows. These are fundamentals that form the continuing core of your walk with God. The better grasp you have on these concepts, the better your whole life will be.

What fundamentals does a Christian never outgrow? One fundamental is that we are to trust God more than we trust our own understanding *(Passage 1)*. Another fundamental is that God wants us to renew our mind and present our body as a living sacrifice *(Passage 2)*. Then there is the concept of grace. Once you are in Christ God does not condemn you *(Passage 3)*.

This Study Guide includes 8 of the most important fundamentals of the Christian life. These do not grow old, they are never shed as being too simplistic in favor of more profound truths. These verses form the backbone of your entire walk with God.

As you *Flicker* them, give them your attention. Ponder how they challenge your values. Open your soul and breath in God's ageless truth. Invest your energy adapting to God's values and you will experience life as God intends it to be experienced.

Organization of the Book

This book takes you through several passages that are fundamental to faith in Christ and helps you decide how your values may differ from His.

The format of this book encourages you to write out what you notice in the passages and respond to God accordingly. Then as you explore these passages, also be alert to notice what you can learn about what God is like.

If you are not familiar with *Flicker Bible Study*, an explanation of the steps and an example of a *Flickered* passage follows.

How To Flicker the Bible

Facts

In the *Facts* panel, make a list of the *Facts* you see in the passage. You don't have to list all the details. Just try and find the main points. You can use the same words as are in the passage. You will usually get somewhere around four to six *Facts*.

Lessons

In the *Lessons* panel, look over the list of facts and see what you can learn from the passage.

- Is there an example to follow?
- Is there a behavior to stop or start?
- Is there a comfort to accept?

Also, consider what you can learn about God from this passage? What does He value? What does He respond to? What pleases Him? You don't have to find a *Lesson* from every verse. Usually you will get one or two *Lessons* from a passage.

Challenges

In the *Challenges* panel, turn each *Lesson* you surfaced into a question that *Challenges* you. Listen for God to speak to you. He may not speak to you through every verse, but He will speak to you. You will normally get the same number of *Challenges* as *Lessons*.

Response

In the *Response* panel, consider what God is saying to you through this passage and decide how you will respond. Write out your *Response* as a two or three sentence prayer.

Be heartfelt and honest with God. If needed, put "training wheels" on your *Response*: "Lord help me to want this." Better to be honest and ask for help, than promise behavior you are not ready to keep.

Example: Psalm 121

To get an idea how to fill in the panels, the following pages present *Psalm 121 Flickered*. This is a guide to help you understand what kind of item goes in each panel.

More items are included in each panel than you would normally write out in the study of a passage. More are included to give you a better idea what goes in each panel.

For more explanation of *Flicker Bible Study* see our book, *Flickering the Bible: Desire-powered Inductive Bible Study*.

Example Passage

Psalms 121:1 I lift up my eyes to the mountains; From where shall my help come?

Psalms 121:2 My help [comes] from the LORD, Who made heaven and earth.

Psalms 121:3 He will not allow your foot to slip; He who keeps you will not slumber.

Psalms 121:4 Behold, He Who keeps Israel Will neither slumber nor sleep.

Psalms 121:5 The LORD is your keeper; the LORD is your shade on your right hand;

Psalms 121:6 The sun will not smite you by day, Nor the moon by night.

Psalms 121:7 The LORD will protect you from all evil; He will keep your soul.

Psalms 121:8 The Lord will guard your going out and your coming in From this time forth and forever. (NASB)

F LCR FACTS

I look up and wonder where my help will come from.

My help comes from God who made heaven and earth

God won't let me fall because He is always watching, He doesn't sleep

He keeps Israel and doesn't sleep or even slumber

The Lord keeps me and shades me at my right hand

The Lord protects me from evil He is keeping my soul safe

FL**CR** LESSONS

There are times we know we need help beyond ourselves

Help comes from God Who created heaven and earth and is alert and ready to help

God is constantly watching, ready to catch me before I fall

He can be so attentive because He never sleep or slumbers

God "keeps" Israel; God "keeps" me. Keeping me means He observes me, guards me, takes care of me, maintains me, retains me in His possession.

FL**CR** CHALLENGES

Am I humble enough to seek help when I need it?

Do I go to God for help, or something else?

Do I trust God to "keep" me?

Am I willing to learn what God considers "falling" instead of assuming falling means failure.

FL**CR** RESPONSES

Lord, help me to be more aware of Your help and presence.

Help me see my relationship with You from Your perspective.

Passage 1—Trust God (Proverbs 3:5-8)

Proverbs 3:5 Trust in the LORD with all your heart And do not lean on your own understanding.

Proverbs 3:6 In all your ways acknowledge Him, And He will make your paths straight.

Proverbs 3:7 Do not be wise in your own eyes; Fear the LORD and turn away from evil.

Proverbs 3:8 It will be healing to your body And refreshment to your bones. (NASB1995)

Trust in the Lord.

If you want to follow a straight path, acknowledge God as your leader.

FLCR CHALLENGES

Do I completely trust God to lead me?

FLCR RESPONSES

Commentary

We have all been at fork in the road where something has gone wrong and we need to make a decision. At that point we have a choice to lean on our own understanding, or trust God and lean on His plan for us. Trust with an undivided heart comes from an allegiance to a God Who has clear promises and a clear perspective. We need to get to know Him before we will be willing to trust Him when things don't make sense.

What does it mean to trust the Lord with "all your heart"? The heart is generally considered the seat of your emotions, but the Bible also uses heart to refer to your will and or your mind. Putting that together, we'll say the heart refers to your whole inner being. Trust the Lord with all your heart would then say to trust Him with no conflicting thoughts or feelings. You would be settled, resolved. Your heart would not be divided between calm and worry. You might be suffering, but you know God will see you through. He knows best. You hold onto God's promises so your heart is settled. You achieve resolve. The only way to have this kind of trust is to know Him and His truth. It is stronger than your fear.

What does it mean "in all your ways acknowledge Him and He will make your paths straight?" To acknowledge someone is to accept the place they have in your life. Acknowledging can also mean to express gratitude. So, if we acknowledge God in all our ways we are saying His existence impacts ALL our ways.

The question is, do we want to be thankful for God's influence, or rebel against it? If we want to be our own boss we will refuse to acknowledge God as our boss. Once we don't acknowledge God, we forfeit His promise to make our path straight. The choice is ours. Acknowledge God in ALL our ways and receive a straight path, or choose our own way and start zig zagging. A straight path is straight (not necessarily "pain free") but it will have the least amount of detours to recover from.

Can respectfully fearing the Lord affect your health? According to this passage, yes! I guess it just makes sense. If you exchange the worry of being your own boss for acknowledging Him as your boss you have less stress and wear and tear on your body! It sounds like healing starts as soon as respect and obedience start. Trusting God is less stressful when you remember He is all powerful, all wise, all holy, all loving, and works all things together for good. His references are better than ours.

What God is Like

- *1. He is protective of His children.* He does not put pressure on us to take care of ourselves. He wants us to trust and obey Him as He leads us. He wants to protect our health.

- *2. He wants to be close with us.* He wants us to acknowledge Him in ALL our ways, not just a few things.

- *3. He is trustworthy!* He wants us to trust Him even if things don't make sense.

- *4. He does what is best for His children.* He leads us in straight paths. His way is the most efficient, with the fewest detours.

Passage 2—Living Sacrifice (Romans 12:1-3)

Romans 12:1 Therefore I urge you, brethren, by the mercies of God, to present your bodies a living and holy sacrifice, acceptable to God, [which is] your spiritual service of worship.

Romans 12:2 And do not be conformed to this world, but be transformed by the renewing of your mind, so that you may prove what the will of God is, that which is good and acceptable and perfect.

Romans 12:3 For through the grace given to me I say to everyone among you not to think more highly of himself than he ought to think; but to think so as to have sound judgment, as God has allotted to each a measure of faith. (NASB1995)

Paul urges...

By the mercies of God...

That we present your bodies to God...

To be a living and holy sacrifice.

God wants us to worship Him by presenting our bodies as a living sacrifice to Him.

FLCR CHALLENGES

Am I willing to present my living body to God to use since it is so clearly God's will?

FLCR RESPONSES

Commentary

Have you ever wondered how to really worship God? What does real worship look like? Well, this passage spells out what God considers real worship. He says real worship is when we present our living bodies to Him to use as He sees fit. What He mostly gets is dead bodies coming His way. He wants living bodies who love and trust Him enough to submit to His path. It is a living sacrifice because we sacrifice the helm of our life and present ourselves to His will. That is holy, spiritual service to God—real worship. A bit different from the person who calls worship coming to church, lifting their hands as they sing a few hymns before they go off to do their own thing—anyone can do that. God does not want us to conform to the world. God wants to transform us.

But, have you ever wondered how transformation happens? Verse 2 says we are transformed by the renewing of our mind! Transformation happens in the mind. The battle is won or lost in our mind. How we think determines what we do and how we feel.

If we believe God's Word (that says He is faithful) we will have more peace as we live our life. On the other hand, if we conform to the world's view (that God is unfaithful) we will feel insecure and frightened at times. Our minds need to be renewed by God's perspective and God's wisdom! The world says *we* need to be "good enough" to make it to heaven. Without this verse we might be tempted to just try and be good without renewing our mind. That will only last a little while because that behavior is not powered by a renewed mind. With this verse we see that God wants our minds renewed through Bible study, before He expects to see genuine behavior change.

Many people worry that God's will will ruin their life. How can they be sure that presenting themselves as a living sacrifice won't be bad? Pretty simple really. He says His will is good, acceptable and perfect. He has even supplied the faith to believe it if you take Him at His Word.

God won't ruin your life if you present yourself to Him but you can ruin your life if you think more highly of yourself than you ought to. If you think more highly of yourself than you should, it tempts you to think you know better than God. That is not sound judgment!

God has provided the faith you need. Lean into it and trust Him to help you find His good, acceptable and perfect will for you.

What God is Like

- *1. He cares deeply for us.* He has a specific will for us. He supplies His mercy and a measure of faith to help us present ourselves to Him. He urges us to do it.

- *2. He does not abuse His power.* He is gentle with us. He does not force us to present ourselves to Him.

- *3. He is clear with us.* He tells us how to worship Him. He tells us how to be transformed.

- *4. He wants us to succeed.* He gives us what we need to succeed. We just have to choose to do it.

Passage 3—No Condemnation (Romans 8:1-4)

Romans 8:1 Therefore there is now no condemnation for those who are in Christ Jesus.

Romans 8:2 For the law of the Spirit of life in Christ Jesus has set you free from the law of sin and of death.

Romans 8:3 For what the Law could not do, weak as it was through the flesh, God [did:] sending His own Son in the likeness of sinful flesh and [as an offering] for sin, He condemned sin in the flesh,

Romans 8:4 so that the requirement of the Law might be fulfilled in us, who do not walk according to the flesh but according to the Spirit. (NASB1995)

FLCR FACTS

There is no condemnation for those in Christ Jesus.

If I am in Christ Jesus, I am safe from condemnation. My behavior is not what keeps me safe. Being in Jesus keeps me safe.

Do I think my good behavior keeps me safe from condemnation?

FLCR RESPONSES

Commentary

There is NO condemnation for those in Christ! Why? Because Christ already suffered the condemnation for us. This is like the law of "double jeopardy" which says a person cannot be tried twice for the same crime. Since Christ already paid the penalty for our sins, and we are in Christ, we won't be condemned. Our good behavior is not what keeps us safe. Being in Christ keeps us safe.

Well, if there is no condemnation for our bad behavior, why should we behave well? Because we will still reap the consequences of bad behavior. Sin, even forgiven sin, complicates our life with extra problems and robs us of eternal rewards. But, worst of all, when we sin we disrespect the Lord and give up feeling close to Him.

As a believer we have the opportunity to live a righteous life–not by keeping the law–but in the power of the Holy Spirit. We don't have the power to produce holiness, but we can, through the Holy Spirit, obey God's will. Those who try to obey God in their own strength will fail. God wants us to depend on Him rather than trying to perform for Him. It takes a while to learn how to transfer self-sufficiency to trust-sufficiency. For those who realize they are in the middle of God's plan, and trust Him to supply what is necessary to do His will, they will find themselves walking according to the Spirit of Christ. The focus is not on your own behavior and what you lack, but on God's promises and ability. So, instead of trying to pump up your faith, look to Jesus. Watch Him through the Scriptures, and faith follows naturally.

What God is Like

- *1. God is righteous.* He did not violate the law of sin and death. He met the requirement of sin and death by sending Christ.

- *2. God is humble.* He was willing to come in the likeness of sinful flesh to help us.

- *3. God really loves and cares for us.* He was willing to lay aside His glory to come and save us.

- *4. God wants to be close to us.* He wants us to walk according to His Spirit.

- *5. God protects us!* He set us free from the law of sin and death.

Passage 4—Consider Trials All Joy (James 1:2-4)

James 1:2 Consider it all joy, my brethren, when you encounter various trials,

James 1:3 knowing that the testing of your faith produces endurance.

James 1:4 And let endurance have [its] perfect result, so that you may be perfect and complete, lacking in nothing. (NASB1995)

Consider it joy when you have various trials.

We can decide how to think about the trials we go through. Instead of despising and resenting them, we can consider them with joy.

How am I thinking about the trials I'm going through? Am I resenting them, or considering them with joy?

Commentary

Have you ever wished you were perfect, lacking nothing? Well, you're on the right track. God says we can be perfect and complete. It has nothing to do with our abilities, and everything to do with our faith in His abilities. Every time we find ourselves going through a difficult time, our faith is being tested. Will we joyfully believe that God is powerful enough to perform His will? If so, we are well on our way to perfection in God's eyes.

But what does it mean to consider the trial a joyful thing? Joy is a spiritual response that grows out of our faith and hope. It stems from a belief that all is well with our soul regardless of the trial. It is different than trying to be happy about the trial. Happiness is tied to feelings of pleasure. Joy stems from the peace of knowing God has our back.

We might not be able to control what happens to us, but we can control how we think about it. If we know the trials are tools in God's Hands, we won't get so worn out fighting them, and our endurance will increase. God says our faith will produce endurance which will make us perfect.

God is not hard to please. He wants us to put our faith in *His* ability and *His* love to take care of what concerns us today. All the tomorrows of our life have to pass by Him, before they get to us. The more we know God and His plan, the more our faith flows which increases our endurance. Endurance might not seem that important until you run out of it!

It is important that we "know" this is how God strengthens us. This thought is not intuitive. When I [D] go to the gym, it is not obvious that I need to stress and tear down my muscles in order to strengthen them. It is the same outside the gym. Trials come and it is not obvious our job is to select our attitude. We can choose to believe the trial is harmful and fight it, or we can choose to be joyful knowing that God can use this for our benefit. Each time we believe God, our faith is strengthened and our endurance increases.

Satan wants us to focus on the trial and be harmed. The trial is not the focus. Faith in God's ability is the focus. As our faith endures God makes us perfect, lacking nothing, because we are counting on God and He is perfect, lacking nothing.

What God is Like

- *1. God is powerful.* He can take what was meant for evil and use it for our good.

- *2. God is in control.* He can help His children get stronger no matter what happens to them.

- *3. God is not hard to please.* He says we are perfect, complete, lacking nothing if our faith rests on Him Who is the One Who is perfect, complete, lacking nothing.

- *4. God values endurance.* He wants us to be strong because we know He is able.

- *5. God asks us to choose our attitude* to focus on Him or to focus on the problem.

Passage 5—God's Sheep (John 10:27-30)

John 10:27 "My sheep hear My voice, and I know them, and they follow Me;

John 10:28 and I give eternal life to them, and they will never perish; and no one will snatch them out of My hand.

John 10:29 "My Father, who has given [them] to Me, is greater than all; and no one is able to snatch [them] out of the Father's hand.

John 10:30 "I and the Father are one." (NASB)

God's sheep hear His voice.

God's sheep hear His voice. It is a certainty. We need to learn to recognize His voice.

Do I recognize God's voice in my life, or am I too distracted to realize when a thought comes from God?

FLCR RESPONSES

Commentary

God's sheep hear His voice. It is said with such certainty. So we ARE hearing, but have we learned to recognize and pay attention to His voice?

We have many thoughts throughout the day. How can we recognize ones that are from God? Well, it has been my [D] experience that God's message usually comes "out of the blue." I might be thinking about something, and then get a thought that surprises me because it seems fresh and not something I was on track to think. Sometimes God's message interrupts other thoughts we are having. It just pops into our head on top of the other thought. God's thoughts are usually not louder than the others, so we have to be listening for them.

Another way to recognize His voice is to read it directly. His word is His voice and He often uses it to speak directly to our current situation.

If we ARE hearing God's voice, how can we miss it? Is it possible our life is so chaotic and noisy that we are too distracted to hear His quiet voice? God is not an obnoxious, loud bully. We can tune Him out, but we will miss His wise counsel.

Verse 27 says that God's sheep follow Him. But, what if you're worried about being able to follow Him? That might mean you have a small view of God, because God is sovereign over His sheep. He knows how to lead them. He is promising that His sheep will never perish. We are safe in God because He is greater than all danger. He is powerful enough to lead us, because *He is able*, not because *we are perfect*. He is more powerful than our sin.

Both God the Father and Jesus watch over and care for their sheep. They are both invested in our welfare. They will see us home. Listen to His voice so your path is straight.

What God is Like

- *1. He is protective of His sheep.* He won't allow any to perish or be kidnapped.

- *2. He is gentle.* His voice is quiet. He does not want to yell to get our attention.

- *3. He shares responsibility with us.* He wants us to make the effort to be quiet so we learn to recognize His voice.

- *4. God is more powerful than our sin.* He can lead us home.

- *5. God is more powerful than evil.* He can protect us from perishing. He won't lose us.

Passage 6—Saved by Grace (Ephesians 2:8-10)

Ephesians 2:8 For by grace you have been saved through faith; and that not of yourselves, [it is] the gift of God;

Ephesians 2:9 not as a result of works, so that no one may boast.

Ephesians 2:10 For we are His workmanship, created in Christ Jesus for good works, which God prepared beforehand so that we would walk in them. (NASB)

You are saved by God's grace.

God provides everything we need for salvation. He has the grace to do it and supplies the faith we need to believe.

FLCR CHALLENGES

Do I realize God provided EVERYTHING I needed for salvation? Do I realize He gave me my faith so I could believe?

FLCR RESPONSES

Commentary

Anyone who is a "giver" knows the joy, freedom and power of giving. Jesus said in *Acts 20:35b* "*It is more blessed to give than receive.*" It is always a blessing to be in a position to give instead of a position of need. So, it is tempting to approach our salvation with the idea of bringing something to it. "God must have picked me because I am pretty moral" or "God appreciates my ability to lead and will use that for His kingdom," or on the other hand, "I'm don't see why God picked me, it feels like a mistake. I'm not very lovable." It is hard to believe it is not about our worthiness. But, sadly, we are so unworthy that God has to provide EVERYTHING we need for salvation! He is in the position of *power* and we are in the position of *need*. He even has to supply the faith we need to believe! Trying to drum up why we are worthy puts our focus on ourselves. God does not want us thinking He saved us as a result of something we have done. No one can boast that they are saved because of their ability.

Our good works have nothing to do with our salvation, but the good works He prepares us for have a lot to do His plans for us.

Have you ever considered the idea that God has created good works just for you? They are all ready. He just wants you to walk in them. We will probably have to access some of the faith He gave us to step out and find our good work "assignments." We are typically gifted to accomplish the good works He wants us to perform. If you are a gifted mechanic, God might use your skills to help widows with their cars. If you are good with hair and makeup, He might have you help out-of-work women learn to look their best for job interviews. Some of you might help them present their resume effectively. We were created to live with God and His other children in harmony. Be on the lookout for your good works. They are already prepared. Use your faith to step into them.

Your life won't make sense until you find the good works that are your purpose.

What God is Like

- *1. God is wildly generous.* He provides everything we need in order to be forgiven. Then He continues to prepare good works for us so we can have purpose as we walk with Him.

- *2. God protects us.* We are created in Christ Jesus.

- *3. God wants us.* He created us. We are His workmanship.

Passage 7—Confess Sin (1 John 1:8-10)

1 John 1:8 If we say that we have no sin, we are deceiving ourselves and the truth is not in us.

1 John 1:9 If we confess our sins, He is faithful and righteous to forgive us our sins and to cleanse us from all unrighteousness.

1 John 1:10 If we say that we have not sinned, we make Him a liar and His word is not in us. (NASB1995)

If we say we have no sin we are deceiving ourselves.

All people sin, even Christians. That is the truth. No exceptions. God wants us to face that.

Do I realize I will always sin?

Commentary

God wants us to be in reality. The reality is we sin. He wants us to confess it. This keeps us close to Him and dependent on Him. He is a diligent kind of Parent, willing to forgive and teach as we walk closely with Him. He never tires of forgiving us but He wants us to be honest with Him, and ourselves, about our sin. He is a dream Parent, willing to be involved in a loving, helpful way.

But, some of us had punitive earthly parents who abused their authority, enforcing rules in a mean-spirited manner. We may read these verses and be leery. For us growing up, it was better to hide our sins, otherwise we were abused. From our point of view it seems like it would be safer to hide our sins from God. We might think "maybe we'll just ignore our sins and hope God does the same thing"? Or, we think, "if we confess, how do we know we're really forgiven? Growing up we got slapped if we didn't have just the right look on our face or tone in our voice. What if we mess up our confession with God?" This approach to God is flawed. There is a better way.

Then others of us had permissive parents who never enforced the rules. They were too distracted with other things to follow up with us. We enjoyed a peer relationship with them instead of a parent/child relationship. At the time, we probably thought we were fortunate to have such cool, hands-off parents. It wasn't until later, when we were in other relationships that we had trouble seeing the part we were contributing to a conflict. We had never been held accountable so now it is hard to recognize our part. It is likely we will have the same problem with God. "Sin? I can't think of any."

God wants us to walk with Him so He can re-Parent us and work on whatever flaws we grew up with. He can help us feel safe to confess. He puts no requirements for forgiveness other than confessing our sins. We don't need to confess perfectly. We don't need to have "just the right look on our face," or "just the right words" to receive forgiveness. God simply says to confess our sins and HE is faithful and WILL forgive our sins. He will help us believe His Word (that we sin) over what we think (I can't think of anything I've done wrong). He wants us to live an intimate, honest life with Him and those around us. We can't be intimate with Him if we are too guarded to be real, or if we think we are self-sufficient and don't need Him.

What God is Like

- • *1. He is patient.* He doesn't mind us bringing Him bad news concerning our sins.

- • *2. He is faithful and kind.* He promises to forgive if we just confess.

- • *3. He cares about the truth and does not want us deceived.*

- • *4. He is a diligent Parent.* He wants close interactions with us.

Passage 8—God So Loved (John 3:16-19)

John 3:16 "For God so loved the world, that He gave His only begotten Son, that whoever believes in Him shall not perish, but have eternal life.

John 3:17 "For God did not send the Son into the world to judge the world, but that the world might be saved through Him.

John 3:18 "He who believes in Him is not judged; he who does not believe has been judged already, because he has not believed in the name of the only begotten Son of God.

John 3:19 "This is the judgment, that the Light has come into the world, and men loved the darkness rather than the Light, for their deeds were evil. (NASB1995)

God loves the world.

God loves the world.

FLCR CHALLENGES

Do I see the heart of God's love for the world?

FLCR RESPONSES

Commentary

God so loved the world. That is the very thing Satan likes to cast doubt about in our mind. "God doesn't love you or this would not have happened." "God is really mad at you and doesn't like you, forget love."

God's love is clear. He sacrificed His only Son's life to save us from condemnation. Satan is the one wrecking the hateful havoc in our life. God wants all His children to be saved from the condemnation that Satan orchestrated when he tempted Adam and Eve. God offers His forgiveness to all.

It is a spectacular intervention. God pays the ultimate price to pay for our sin and just asks us to admit our sin and accept Christ's payment. He does the heavy lifting, while we admit our need for the help.

There will always be those who don't want to admit their need for help. Christ came as Light into the world and they loved darkness instead because it exposed their sin. They choose to stay condemned because they love their sinful activities.

There is no sin too great for God to forgive. Christ's blood is priceless. It can pay the price for any sin. We just have to admit our need and accept God's solution for our forgiveness.

What God is Like

- *1. God is a Giver.* He gives to the point of sacrifice.

- *2. God is relational.* His relationship and love for us moves Him to sacrifice for us.

- *3. God is the compassionate Judge.* Even though He is the Judge of the world, His purpose in coming to the world was not to judge it. His purpose was to save it from judgement.

"Am I wise
in my own
eyes?"

the Authors

Appendix A
Answers

More answers are given below than you are expected to find when you study the passages. Most people find four to six *Facts,* one or two *Lessons,* one or two *Challenges,* and one *Response* when they study a passage. Extra answers are given here to help you better recognize *Facts, Lessons, Challenges,* and *Responses.*

Chapter 1—Trust God (Proverbs 3:5-8)

Facts

- Trust in the Lord.
- With all your heart.
- Don't lean on your own understanding.
- In all your ways acknowledge Him.
- He will make your paths straight
- Don't be wise in your own eyes.
- Fear the Lord.
- Turn away from evil.
- It will heal your body.
- It will refresh your bones.

Lessons

- If you want to follow a straight path, acknowledge God as your leader.
- Acknowledge Him in everything you do and He will make your path straight.
- God does not want us to be wise in our own eyes thinking we are self-sufficient and can lean on (support) ourselves. He does not want us to trust our own reasoning over trusting Him. He wants us to trust Him even when things don't make sense and we don't understand.
- God wants us to fear Him, reverence Him, and be in awe of Him, so that we respect Him enough to turn from evil.
- If we trust God with all our heart, we will have less stress which will refresh our bones and heal our body.

Challenges

- Do I completely trust God to lead me?
- Am I acknowledging God as Lord over all my life?
- Am I being wise in my own eyes?
- Am I leaning on my own understanding or am I willing to trust God when things don't make sense to me?
- Do I fear, or respect God enough to turn from evil?

- Do I see how trusting God completely and not leaning on my own understanding is less stressful?
- Do I see how trusting God completely is good for my health?

Responses

- Father, thank You for being trustworthy.
- Thank You for being wise.
- Please forgive me when I start leaning on my own understanding instead of acknowledging You as my Lord.
- Please help me to trust You completely, even when things don't make sense. I want to follow You in straight paths.

Chapter 2—Living Sacrifice (Romans 12:1-3)

Facts

- Paul urges...
- By the mercies of God...
- That we present your bodies to God...
- To be a living and holy sacrifice.
- This is acceptable to God.
- This is your spiritual service of worship.
- God doesn't want us to conform to the world.
- Rather, we should be transformed by the renewing of our mind.
- This will help us know the will of God.
- God's will is good and acceptable and perfect.
- Paul exhorts us through the grace given to him.
- He exhorts us not to think more highly of ourself than we ought.
- Instead, think using sound judgment.
- God has given each a measure of faith.

Lessons

- God wants us to worship Him by presenting our bodies as a living sacrifice to Him. This is seen as holy, spiritual worship. If we want to do something that is God's will, and worship Him at the same time, this is it. It is only by His mercy that we are able to present ourselves to Him. He made the way by His mercies, He has Paul urging us, He really wants this. It is reasonable.

- God does not want us to conform to the world. He wants to transform us to be like Him. This transformation does not start by trying to behave better. It starts with renewing our mind so that we know God, and start to understand His perspective. Then our behavior gradually changes to conform to Him.

- God's will is good, acceptable and perfect. We should not fear God's will for us. It is good.

- God wants us to have sound judgment when evaluating our abilities. He does not want us taking credit for what He enables so that we feel self-sufficient and work without Him. God's grace has supplied the measure of faith that we need to successfully work with Him.

Challenges

- Am I willing to present my living body to God to use since it is so clearly God's will?

- Do I think I can effectively worship God, and at the same time, withhold offering myself to Him?

- Am I conforming to the world or to God?

- Do I want to be transformed, or am I satisfied with how I am now?

- Do I realize transformation comes through my mind?

- Am I trying to transform myself by just trying to behave better?

- Am I finding God's will because my mind is being renewed by God's Word?

- Do I believe God's will for me is good, acceptable and perfect, or do I think He wants to ruin my life?

- Do I realize there is a problem with being self-sufficient and thinking too highly of myself? Do I see it cuts me off from God?

- Do I want to use sound judgment?

- Am I using the measure of faith that God has given me to believe this?

Responses

- Father, thank You for being so clear with what You want from me.

- Thank You that You are good and that Your will is good, acceptable and perfect.

- Thank You for wanting me.

Chapter 3—No Condemnation (Romans 8:1-4)

Facts

- There is no condemnation for those in Christ Jesus.

- The law of the Spirit of life in Christ Jesus...

- ...Has set you free from the law of sin and of death

- What the Law could not do,

- Weak as it was through the flesh,

- God did by sending His own Son in the likeness of sinful flesh.

- He was sent as an offering for sin.

- He condemned sin in the flesh.

- So that the requirement of the Law was fulfilled in us–

- Who do not walk according to the flesh, but according to the Spirit.

Lessons

- If I am in Christ Jesus, I am safe from condemnation. My behavior is not what keeps me safe. Being in Jesus keeps me safe.

- There is a law of life and a law of death. Our sin keeps us under the law of death. The law of life requires that we be righteous. Those who accept Christ as Savior walk in His Spirit and qualify because He is righteous. The Spirit of Christ Jesus sets us free from the law of death and transfers us to the law of life in Christ Jesus. We are no longer condemned to death because of our sin.

Challenges

- Do I think my good behavior keeps me safe from condemnation?

- Am I trusting the work of Jesus to keep me from condemnation?

- Do I feel free from the law of death and alive in the law of life in Christ Jesus?

- Am I thankful for Christ's payment for my sin because I'm no longer under the law of sin and death?

- Am I taking advantage of my ability to walk according to the Spirit of Christ?

Responses

- Thank You Father for sending Christ to set me free from the law of sin and death.

- Please help me to take full advantage of the opportunity to walk according to Your Spirit and find the freedom of life in You.

Chapter 4—Consider Trials All Joy (James 1:2-4)

Facts

- Consider it joy,

- Brothers and sisters,

- When you have various trials.

- Knowing:

- ...that the testing of your faith

- ...produces endurance.

- Let: (cause it to happen)

- ...endurance have its

- ...perfect result.

- So you may be:

- ...perfect,

- ...complete,

- ...lacking in nothing.

Lessons

- We can decide how to think about the trials we go through. Instead of despising and resenting them, we can consider them with joy since they can increase our endurance of faith which will make us feel better and make us perfect in God's eyes.

- We will have various trials. We can't avoid trials no matter how well-behaved we are. They are for our good.

- This passage is addressed to brothers and sisters in Christ. Only God's children should consider trials with joy. God can take what is stressful and hard and use it to increase our faith and make us stronger.

- We can "know" that testing our faith will increase our endurance by "letting" the endurance make us perfect. We have to believe God so that we will cooperate with His training plan. Our faith is continually tested during a trial. Each time we believe God with joy our faith is strengthened and our endurance increases.

- Endurance of faith can make us perfect, complete, lacking nothing in God's eyes. God can be completely satisfied with us when our faith rests on Him. We won't lack anything then because He is perfect, lacking nothing.

Challenges

- How am I thinking about the trials I'm going through? Am I resenting them, or considering them with joy?

- Do I accept that I can't avoid some trials?

- Do I believe that God can increase the endurance of my faith if I keep considering my trials with joy?

- Do I see how enduring faith makes me perfect in God's eyes? Am I putting my effort in the right place?

- Am I cooperating with God's training plan to strengthen my faith?

- Am I willing to keep considering my trials with joy because it will strengthen my endurance of faith?

- Do I see how increasing the endurance of my faith will make my life perfect, complete, lacking nothing in God's eyes?

Responses

- Lord, thank you for giving me the freedom to control my attitude and perspective.

- Thank You for having the power to increase my endurance as I choose to consider my trials with joy because of what You are doing.

Chapter 5—God's Sheep (John 10:27-30)

Facts

- My sheep hear My voice.
- I know them.
- They follow Me.
- I will give them eternal life.
- They will never perish.
- No one will snatch them out of My Hand.
- My Father gave them to Me.
- My Father is greater than all.
- No one can snatch them out of His Hand.
- I and the Father are One.

Lessons

- God's sheep hear His voice. It is a certainty. We need to learn to recognize His voice.

- God knows His sheep. We do not get lost in the herd. He is invested in each one.

- God's sheep follow Him. God is sovereign and knows how to lead His sheep.

- God's sheep will never perish or be kidnapped. There are forces who would like to snatch away God's sheep from Him. We are safe in God because He is greater than all danger.

- God the Father gave Jesus His sheep. The Father and Jesus are One so they share us.

Challenges

- Do I recognize God's voice in my life, or am I too distracted to realize when a thought comes from God?

- Do I really believe that God knows me, or do I think I'm lost in the herd?

- Am I worried about being able to follow God? Do I think I can mess up His ability to lead me? Can I take comfort in God's ability to lead me as I listen for Him?

- Do I realize how safe I am with God? He promises I will never die or get kidnapped by evil. Can I rest in Him because He is greater than all danger?

- Can I see how both God the Father and Jesus watch over and care for their sheep? They are both invested in my welfare.

Responses

- Thank You so much Lord for speaking to me.
- I need Your guidance and wisdom.
- Please help me to recognize Your voice distinctly from my own thoughts.

Chapter 6—Saved by Grace (Ephesians 2:8-10)

Facts

- You are saved by God's grace.
- God gives you faith and salvation as a gift.
- He saves you because of the faith He gave you.
- You are not saved as a result of your own works.
- No one can boast that they are saved by their own works.
- We are created by God.
- We are created in Christ Jesus.
- We are created for good works.
- God prepared the good works for us beforehand.
- He wants us to walk in the good works.

Lessons

- God provides everything we need for salvation. He has the grace to do it and supplies the faith we need to believe.
- God does not want us to boast that we were saved as a result of our own works so He provides everything we need to be saved.
- God created us for good works. He has already prepared the good works for us. He wants us to walk in the good works.
- We were created by God. He created us IN Christ Jesus.

Challenges

- Do I realize God provided EVERYTHING I needed for salvation? Do I realize He gave me my faith so I could believe?
- Do I occasionally think I am worthy in some way for my salvation?
- Do I realize God created me for good works that He has already prepared for me?
- Am I using the faith that He has given me to find and walk in the good works He has prepared for me?
- Do I live and walk like I was made by God?
- Am I living and walking in the reality of being in Christ Jesus or do I just notice the world?

Responses

- Father, thank You so much for Your amazing grace to give me everything I need for salvation.
- Thank You for giving me the faith I need to believe.
- May I keep accessing that faith as I walk with You.

Chapter 7—Confess Sin (1 John 1:8-10)

Facts

- If we say we have no sin we are deceiving ourselves.
- The truth is not in us.
- If we confess our sins,
- He is faithful.
- He is righteous.
- He will forgive our sins.
- He will cleanse us from all sins.
- If we say we have not sinned...
- ...we make Him a liar,
- ...His Word is not in us.

Lessons

- All people sin, even Christians. That is the truth. No exceptions. God wants us to face that. He wants us to confess our sins to Him, and take responsibility for them. He will forgive and cleanse us because He is faithful and righteous.
- God puts no requirements for forgiving Christians, other than confessing our sins to Him. We don't need to confess perfectly. We don't need to have "just the right look" on our face, or "just the right words" to receive forgiveness. God says HE is faithful and WILL forgive our sins if we confess them to Him.
- We need to believe God's Word over what we think. If we have His Word in us, it will keep us from believing things contrary to His Word.

Challenges

- Do I realize I will always sin?
- Am I humble enough to be accountable to God for my sin?
- Am I willing to admit my sin to God or do I try to ignore it or blame it on someone else?
- Do I worry I'm not really forgiven even though I have asked God for forgiveness?
- Am I willing to believe God that I am forgiven if I just confess to Him?
- Am I willing to believe His Word over what I think?
- If I go with what I think over what He says in His Word, do I realize I'm calling God a liar?
- Do I have His Word in me to correct my thinking?

Responses

- Father, thank You for facing the fact that I will sin and for still wanting a relationship with me!
- Thank You for making the way for my sins to be forgiven.
- Please help me to face my sin and come to You confessing it.
- I want to be accountable to You.
- Thank You for being faithful and righteous with me.

Chapter 8—God So Loved (John 3:16-19)

Facts

- God so loved the world, that,
- He gave,
- His only Son, that,
- Whoever believes in Him,
- Would not perish,
- But, would have eternal life.
- God did not send the Son into the world to condemn the world.
- But to save the world.
- Through Jesus, He who believes in Him is not condemned.
- He who does not believe is already condemned, because, He does not believe in God's only Son.
- This is the condemnation: The Light came into the world, but men loved darkness rather than Light because their deeds were evil.

Lessons

- God so loves the world.
- God's response to seeing our condemnation and loving us, was to give His only Son to save us.
- God's gift of salvation is for anyone who believes in Christ's payment for them and wants it.
- God did not send Christ to condemn us, we were already condemned. Christ came to save us.
- Christ is the Light that came into the world.
- Those who love darkness hate the Light because their deeds are evil and light exposes them.

Challenges

- Do I see the heart of God's love for the world?
- Do I realize I was condemned and in peril before I accepted Christ's payment for my sins?
- Do I see how God offers salvation to all who want forgiveness instead of their dark sin?
- Do I live like Christ came to save me, not condemn me?
- Do I share Christ as the world's Light and hope?
- Do I continually choose Christ over sin?

Responses

- Father, thank You for loving us enough to save us from condemnation when we didn't first acknowledge that we were in trouble.
- Thank You for loving the world enough to send Your only Son to pay the price of forgiveness and warn us of our need.
- It is a spectacular gift where You pay the price, and we admit our sin and accept Christ's payment for it.
- You are a positive, loving, generous God Who sent Christ to save us when we were condemned already.

"Christ's
blood can
pay the price
for any sin."

the Authors

www.ingramcontent.com/pod-product-compliance
Lightning Source LLC
Chambersburg PA
CBHW020519030426
42337CB00011B/463